PENGUIN BOOKS

HOLD ON TO YOUR DREAMS

Born in Kasauli (Himachal Pradesh) in 1934, Ruskin Bond grew up in Jamnagar (Gujarat), Dehradun, New Delhi and Simla. His first novel, *The Room on the Roof*, which was written when he was seventeen, received the John Llewellyn Rhys Memorial Prize in 1957. Since then, he has written over 500 short stories, essays, novellas (including *The Adventures of Rusty* and *The Room of Many Colours*) and more than seventy books for children.

He received the Sahitya Akademi Award for English writing in India in 1992, the Padma Shri in 1999 and the Padma Bhushan in 2014. He lives in Landour, Mussoorie, with his extended family.

Ruskin Bond

READ MORE BY RUSKIN BOND

RUSKIN BOND

Hold On To Your Dreams

A LETTER TO YOUNG FRIENDS

Illustrations by Pearl D'Souza

PENGUIN BOOKS

An imprint of Penguin Random House

PENGUIN BOOKS

Penguin Books is an imprint of the Penguin Random House group of companies
whose addresses can be found at global.penguinrandomhouse.com

Published by Penguin Random House India Pvt. Ltd
4th Floor, Capital Tower 1, MG Road,
Gurugram 122 002, Haryana, India

Penguin
Random House
India

First published in Penguin Books by Penguin Random House India 2024

ISBN 9780143468998

Book design and layout by Samar Bansal
Typeset in Bakeshop Light
Printed at Thomson Press India Ltd, New Delhi

www.penguin.co.in

MIX
Paper | Supporting
responsible forestry
FSC® C010615

This letter is for older readers, too.
If it's hot, enjoy the shade.
If it's cold, enjoy the sunshine.
But don't stop dreaming.

My dear young friends,

It's no use asking me for advice. I seldom took any, and when I did, it was usually the wrong kind. Besides, young people usually resent being given advice by patronizing elders and go out of their way to do the very opposite of what they have been advised to do.

You will learn from your mistakes. Or maybe you won't. I keep making the same mistakes. I don't learn from them. I see other people making mistakes and learning very little from them.

The human being was born to make mistakes. It was probably a mistake on the part of the

Creator or on the part of evolution, whichever is your preference. The great philosophers, scientists and men of religion have all tried to justify our presence on this planet. And to what end? Conflict. Human conflict caused by the same territorial greed that is found in animals.

In many ways, the human is a superior sort of animal but only to a small degree. I look at my cat, Mimi, basking in the sun. She is elegant and beautiful to behold—superior to a dog, definitely. She does not fawn over humans because she sees through them. She knows my weaknesses and that, as a human, I am supposed to have a conscience.

~~THE~~

~~HUMAN BEING~~

~~WAS BORN~~

~~TO MAKE~~

~~MISTAKES.~~

My eyesight is terribly poor now, and one sunny morning, book in hand, I sat down in my easy chair, only to rise immediately, for I had sat on Mimi! She shrieked in anguish, for I am no lightweight. I apologized humbly and took my book elsewhere, leaving her the sole occupant of the easy chair.

Now, the chair belongs to her. She occupies it by right and gives me a stern look if I approach. Other men might have acted differently—picked her up and thrown her out of the window—but she knows me well. She knows that I have a conscience, something that animals don't possess. Mimi has no conscience. She will torture a mouse before putting it to death. Some humans are like that, too. Being more animal than human, they take pleasure in torturing their own kind. The distinction between humans and animals can be miniscule.

Mimi can't make bombs. Some humans make bombs so that other humans can use them.

The distinction between humans and animals can be miniscule.

All that human intelligence going into the making of something that will one day finish off the human race. But are we worth preserving? One wouldn't think so, judging by the way we do our best to annihilate each other . . .

✳ ✳ ✳

I broke off there, partly because I was being summoned to breakfast and partly because I was getting into a depression and wanted to avoid it.

I am a cheerful and optimistic person by nature. Still, occasionally—once or twice a year—I get the feeling that everything I've done and written, all those hundreds of books and stories and notebooks full of words, are utterly useless, frivolous and doomed to obscurity. I tell myself I would have been better employed doing something else. But doing what? My choices are limited.

'I could sell boiled eggs,' I tell myself wryly, 'like those unlettered but good folk from the nearby villages, selling boiled eggs to tourists on the Mall Road.'

Boiling an egg is something I can still do. One must give the customer a little salt and pepper to go with the egg and serve it on a piece of newspaper. But it's getting cold on the

Mall Road nowadays, and I doubt if I could stay up late with those hardy egg-sellers.

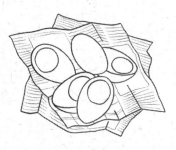

There's a genius I know who makes wonderful omelettes, selling them from his tiny shop. He is a humble person who always greets me as I pass by. I wish my stories were as good as his omelettes. I wish I could make a decent omelette. I have tried to, from time to time, but they always turn out to be too thin or squishy.

101 Failed Omelettes could be a good title for my autobiography.

'Never despair. But if you do, then work on in despair.' I read that somewhere when I was a schoolboy and made a note of it. I've tried to live up to the sentiment through all these years of success and failure, alternating with the seasons, or so it seems. Something to do with the rhythms of life, I feel. For a time, everything goes well, and then things go awry, and one is left struggling against the current.

'There is a tide in the affairs of men,' wrote Shakespeare, 'which, taken at the flood, leads on to fortune.' But first, one must know which

'**NEVER DESPAIR**. But if you do, then **WORK ON IN DESPAIR**'

...*way the tide is running* Mr W. Shakespeare did say a lot of good things.

* * *

'In the still of the night...' The lyrics of this old Cole Porter song run through my mind as I look out of my window when the occasional Diwali rocket lights up the darkness.

Not many fireworks this year, but some hotels and schools are lit up. We haven't put up lights at the house this year, as Prem, an old friend and companion, passed on last month after a long struggle with diabetes and related disorders.

Every Diwali (and New Year), I try to write a few lines in the morning, a sort of rehearsal for the year ahead. It's a superstition of mine. I'm full of superstitions, although I pretend to be a rational person. A big horseshoe—given to me by an old lady fifty years ago—went missing last month, and I was quite upset. I'm sure it's somewhere in the house, though. The carpenters must have moved it when they were repairing the windows and the front door. It will turn up—nobody wants my old horseshoe. Like my poems, the horseshoe isn't saleable.

I have written my few words for Diwali this year. After two cold, foggy days, the sun is out, and my backache has gone. Sunshine is a great healer.

Putting down my thoughts and reflections in the form of a letter comes readily to me than using the more formal medium of a memoir or the egoism of a journal. In a journal, one is talking to oneself. I'd rather be talking to someone else—someone on the same wavelength, so to speak—a reader like myself or a friend from long ago who is far away.

The first diary or journal I kept when I was just out of school—some seventy years ago—

became my first novel, The Room on the Roof. It belonged to a particular time and place. In it, I was going back and forth between phases of my life; the past was hardly over, and the future was unknown. Now, it's all past, and there are many stories and episodes. But the future is still unknown—if indeed there is a future—which I rather doubt.

I am lucky to be here after all these years, still putting words to paper, even if I go off the page from time to time. The advantage of writing by hand is that you can put your nose to the pad and locate the position of the lines.

I am lucky that I can still read and write, communicate with you, enjoy the sunshine,

The advantage of writing by hand is that you can put your nose to the pad and locate the position of the lines.

walk about (a bit unsteadily), eat and drink most of the things I like, and watch old movies on the big screen in the dining room. But watching an old film (or even a new one) on YouTube isn't the same as watching it in a cinema. Somehow, at home, the magic is gone, and I am distracted by other things.

During the lonely years of my boyhood, the cinema was my great escape. I could sit in a darkened hall and forget reality for an hour or two. I could be a tap dancer or a pirate or a cowboy or even a great singer! I couldn't sing or dance, and I was afraid of swords and guns, but I could write a little. In the end, it was the words that took over and provided me with my real escape, a permanent one, secure and happy in a world of words—the printed word, hard to eradicate, always beside me, answering my summons.

Listen to the sound of silence.

The fireworks are over, and the merrymakers have left. Silence descends on the mountain. But there is never complete silence. I can hear the singing of crickets on the hillside, the distant barking of a dog, and the exuberant whistle of a bulbul perched on the light pole opposite my window. But these are natural sounds. They blend with the brooding presence of the mountain; they do not intrude on one's thoughts and pleasant reverie. They are unlike loud car horns, the grinding of gears, the thunder of motorcycles, the drone of helicopters, the noise of wedding bands or preachers on loudspeakers.

LISTEN TO THE SOUND OF

S
I
L
E
N
C
E

Man-made sounds are intrusive, except when they aspire to great music. Even then, a poor singer can destroy a good song. Of course, there are some mundane sounds that do not intrude because they are part of our daily lives. Like the plonk of newspapers as they land on the front door, the rattle of teacups from the kitchen, the call of the milkman, the clatter of children's shoes as they run down the road—late for school!

We do not resent these sounds; we barely notice them—any more than we notice the hiss of steam from a kettle or water dripping from a tap until it is turned off.

I sit here in silence, waiting for the first sounds of the morning. The crickets are still at it. They do make a lot of noise, considering their size.

Mimi hates the sound of crackers and other fireworks, especially those ear-shattering 'bombs'. She hides under a chair or bed until the explosion sounds subside. Most animals hate the sound of guns and fireworks going off. A sense of self-preservation makes them run for cover.

Only the human species has a fascination for the destructive qualities of gunpowder. We progressed from chemical bombs to atom and hydrogen bombs, and now we have nuclear devices of unimaginable destructive powers. It has been almost eighty years since atomic bombs were dropped on Hiroshima and Nagasaki. Now, once again, the world's most powerful nations are revving up for another universal conflict with no shortage of weaponry for the coming events. All history is a chronicle of one nation wanting to grab another's land and wealth, a philosophy that hasn't changed. And so, the bigger the bomb, the better off you are dealing with your envious neighbour.

ONLY THE HUMAN SPECIES HAS A FASCINATION FOR THE  **destructive** QUALITIES OF GUNPOWDER.

In 2023 and 2024, the bombs fell in Ukraine and Palestine. I am convinced this pattern will continue. These bombs will keep falling until there is a general conflagration, and even AI (artificial intelligence) won't be able to stop it.

Mimi is wise to hide under a bed (when Diwali bombs go off). The survivors will be those who have holes to hide in—skunks and rabbits, snakes and scorpions, bugs and beetles, beavers and foxes and other burrowing animals. Earthworms, too.

When all is gone,

The worm will turn,

And a new species will be born.

WHEN ALL IS GONE,

THE WORM WILL TURN,

AND A NEW SPECIES

WILL BE BORN.

And on that pessimistic note, I will rest my pen and head for breakfast. At least, the hens are still laying eggs.

* * *

Do I never tire of writing, you ask.

The written word has enabled me to conquer both time and distance. With its help, I can recall scenes from my boyhood, my friends and familiars, lost loves, moments of joy, anguish, triumphs and tragedies—the world around me! Everything from the bluebird on the wing to the deer at the mountain stream.

When I recollect the books I read, I remember how their words, their prosody, took me to faraway places, remote times and distant days—the London of Dickens, the Russia of Dostoyevsky, the France of Balzac and Baudelaire, the America of Mark Twain and O. Henry, the Japan of Lady Murasaki, the China of Lao-Tzu, the India of Kalidas and Tagore, the Persia of Nafiz and Firdausi, the Greece of Homer, the Spain of Cervantes, the Scotland of Burns and the Ireland of Yeats.

I can speak to you better through these words than by telephone or photographs, for our thoughts are invisible and can only be captured by the magic of the written word.

Sometimes, when ideas dry up, words don't flow and the surroundings—familiar or otherwise—fail to inspire. At such times, it's best to stop writing for a while, just for a few days. Instead, go for long walks—in the town or the outskirts—until you tire of walking. Once you have done that, you will be happy to return to your desk or easy chair and take up your pen again.

I can speak to you better through these words than by telephone or photographs, for our thoughts are invisible and can only be captured by the magic of the written word.

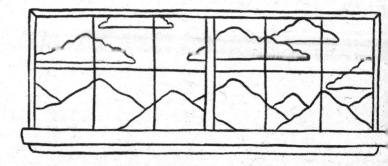

I used to do that when I was younger—walk everywhere. But now, on the verge of ninety, I find it difficult to walk more than a few paces up the road, and I need someone with me to make sure I don't walk into a ditch. So, instead of walking, I turn to a book or watch an old movie (my childhood escape, as you would remember) or look out of the window at the cloud formations and the changing light on the mountains.

Do I tire of writing? No. These words are my lifeblood. They have made it possible for me to live the life I wanted to live. And here I am, in my dotage, still stringing them together.

Besides, there are compensations. Like Emerson, I am a great believer in the law of compensation. All those years of hard work have made life a little easier for me now. And if, in the process, my eyesight has been affected, well, it means I no longer fall in love at first sight, with all the complications that ensue!

Make no mistake, though: writing is a solitary art, a lonely profession, whichever way you look at it. You are on your own, even if you are

Do I tire
of writing?
No.
These words are
my lifeblood.

a member of a large family or a schoolteacher amidst hundreds of noisy children (or you might be one of those children wanting to write!) or an inmate of a crowded jail. You are alone in a crowd, and you need that loneliness because you have to communicate with yourself and explore the inner sanctum of your mind.

Loneliness becomes part of a writer's being. O. Henry spent two years in prison on a charge of forgery. He met all sorts of people, from small crooks to big-time financiers, and when he'd completed his sentence, did O. Henry seek the bright lights and the party scene? No, he rented a small room in a ramshackle part of New York, and there he churned out two or three stories a week for the dailies—stories that brought him a few dollars, just sufficient for his needs; stories that we still read today, over a hundred years since they were written. These were stories about good people, old people, all sorts of people (for he had seen them all) and all written out of loneliness, the loneliness of a writer who had been part of the crowd and yet not a part of it. He had been on the inside, looking out, whereas now he was on the inside, looking in.

Loneliness doesn't always lead to great writing or, sometimes, any kind of writing. The absence of human company, someone to

LONELINESS BECOMES PART OF A WRITER'S BEING.

hold your hand, can result in depression and an escape from reality into alcohol or drugs. Humans, like monkeys, are gregarious by nature and are inclined to go off their heads if left alone for too long. Cats, like Mimi, are not gregarious. They are quite happy to be left alone. If Mimi can have possession of my easy chair, she will spread herself in it for half the day, only rousing for a sardine or a sausage. But unlike Garfield, the cartoon cat, Mimi is a fussy eater and will turn up her nose at pastries and pizzas.

I love solitude. Not so much because it helps me to write, but because it enables me to look at

Humans, like monkeys, are gregarious by nature and are inclined to go off their heads if left alone for too long.

the world around me in a more intimate way—following the flight of an eagle, the changing patterns of the clouds, the cows grazing on the hillside and the girl calling to them to come home, the grass springing up on the steps—each blade of grass important in itself, each blade of grass representing the entirety of nature, for if grass cannot grow on this earth, nothing else can.

I concentrate on that blade of grass; I become one with it. I must try writing like grass—springing up in different places, renewing itself, becoming more grass, green and growing. The rose fades, the poppy dies, but the grass lives on. The flowers in our garden perish, but the grass survives.

It is good to be alone sometimes, but don't go searching for solitude, lest it turn into loneliness. When I first came to these hills, I rented a small cottage near the forest. It was a lovely place. I had an owl and a bat for company. I wrote a poem about each of them, but that was it. I became restless, unable to sit at my desk for long. The words weren't coming! So, I took a walk, a long walk and stopped at a wayside teashop for refreshment. The shopkeeper was a friendly fellow, and he needed company, too. We soon got talking. He told me his story, and I told him mine. Later, when I got home, I wrote

THE ROSE FADES,
THE POPPY DIES,
BUT THE GRASS
LIVES ON.

about our encounter. It was a joyful piece of writing. Owls and bats are fine, but we need people, too.

✳ ✳ ✳

When you are in your teens or twenties (as some of you might be), the world stretches before you, and life is full of possibilities. And that is how it should be. But when you are ninety, what is there to look forward to? And is there anything left to get out of life? One has achieved all that one has set out to achieve—no, not all, but a few good things— and the limitations of old age make further achievements problematic. One has done one's best. Now, it is time to rest.

But there is no rest for some of us. We are not satisfied with what we have done; we want to do more and do it better. This is not reasonable, but then, is man reasonable? He may be rational, but reasonable? Not by a long chalk. He is unreasonable as a child, and as an old man, he is just as stubborn and unpredictable. An American president is determined to run again for the same high office. His opponent is likely to be an ex-president, just three or four years younger, notorious for his childish ways and John Wayne personality. But they are politicians, and politicians the world over are known for their reluctance to give up the trappings of power.

You and I are not politicians, my friends. Nor do we wish to take up golf or grow tomatoes in our backyards. But we will do something. We won't give up so easily.

So, with the morning sun alighting on this writing pad, I write a few lines to you, boys and girls, men and women, telling you something about my life, its highlights, low lights, sunlight and its twilight, and in doing so, perhaps, help you a little on your journey.

It is never an easy way, no matter how favourable the circumstances are. Inherited wealth can destroy a man just as easily as extreme poverty. I think now of my stepfather, who inherited a good business, run it into the ground, and spent most of his life fleeing creditors and the income tax department. On the other hand, there was a penniless refugee from Sindh who worked in a sugar factory, mastered the business, and went on to own and run several sugar factories.

I am no businessman, and I have never aspired to take great risks. Still, I have always believed that good work should be rewarded. I can reflect on my long writing life and boast that I have always been paid for my work. I have always insisted on it, whether it was just five rupees when I was a boy or a few thousand when I was older.

I sold my first story for five rupees. I was just out of school at the time, and I celebrated by going to the pictures and treating myself to a banana split in the Kwality restaurant in Dehradun's up-market shopping centre.

Five rupees went a long way in those halcyon days. There was enough left over for a comic paper after my little splurge. And when, a few months later, I sold a story for fifty rupees. I felt I'd made a fortune! And in a way, I had. Our first earnings are always the most memorable. The thrill of receiving that first pay packet, money order or cheque—how can one forget it? That feeling isn't quite the same today, seventy years later, because I have sold hundreds of stories. But now the thrill comes from the writing, the satisfaction I get from doing a good piece of work. And if it pleases a reader, one or many, that is as good a reward as any material recompense.

As a boy, I wrote for myself. Now, I write for myself, my reader, my publisher and my family! I can't stop, no matter how old I get.

And you must never stop doing the thing that has made it possible for you to live the life of your choosing. Carry on doing the thing that gives you joy. Don't stop!

Although I don't see too well, I have written these few pages this morning. The sun is still on this page. Once it moves, I will brush my teeth, shave and enjoy my breakfast. Usually, it's a fried egg, but today I will treat myself to a 'rumble-tumble' (that's what my father used to call it)—an egg-bhurji beaten up with chillies, onions and tomatoes. Then, I will read a little in the sunroom with Mimi, surrounded by flowering geraniums. They flower all year round in this little room, a miniature greenhouse.

* * *

When you are young, travel alone. When you are old, travel with a companion.

In our twilight years, we need someone to lean on a little—a son, daughter, grandchild, partner or an old friend. The life I have today would not be possible if it were not for family.

When I was eighteen, I lived alone in London for a couple of years. I did not look after myself very well and suffered for it. But at that age, one recovers quickly from physical ailments and the body's neglect. Returning to India, I was on my own for nearly three years. I was even more neglectful but young enough and resilient enough to manage occasional disorders—stomach upsets, jaundice and poor eyesight.

When I came to live in the hills, I was once again on my own during the early years, but lungfuls of clean air and the active use of my legs—walking everywhere instead of relying on wheels—kept me in reasonable shape. Mind, it is said, can overcome matter, but I think it would be equally valid to say that matter can influence the mind. If I am writing fluently this morning, it is because I do not have a headache or a backache or a troublesome itch that refuses to go away.

The mind is all-powerful, but matter can undermine the mind. A truth many great writers discovered when alcohol, drugs and

MIND CAN

OVERCOME

MATTER

———————————

MATTER CAN

INFLUENCE

THE MIND

other forms of self-indulgence took a toll on their creative process. From Edgar Alan Poe to Hemmingway, Dylan Thomas and scores of other gifted writers, their dependence on strong drinks drove them to despair and a premature demise. Enjoy the good things of life, dear friends, but do not become a slave to anything.

I am fortunate to have a family—one that has grown around me by chance, circumstance and loving providence. When Prem and his family started living with me more than sixty years ago, little did I know that his children and grandchildren would become my children and grandchildren. I am surrounded by family. Prem's eldest son, Rakesh, his wife Beena and their children— Siddharth, Shrishti and Gautam—are my family. The three are no longer children. Shrishti, who fusses over me the most, was with me yesterday. She was telling me about her plans of selling village products in the cities.

I am not alone, except in my thoughts and on paper. There is always someone to hold my hand, to lead me down our crooked steps, to make me comfortable, to take me for a long drive, to see that I am well and warm at night.

For the nights can be difficult. Sleep does not always come easily. I lie awake thinking, and after two to three hours of thoughts—thoughts of the past and for the future—I fall into a disturbed sleep; a sleep full of vivid dreams, some disturbing and some so pleasant that I wish they had not ended. But when the dream ends, so does everything else.

Hold on to your dreams, dear friends. I mean your daydreams—the dreams you have had since you were a child. They sustain you through the difficult years, the struggles and disappointments.

Hold on to your dreams. Don't let them go. Dream great, dream beautiful. Build castles in the air. And put foundations under them.

*** *** ***

I have no wish to lecture you. God forbid! You have probably received your fair share of lectures from parents, teachers, principals, employers, motivational speakers and self-appointed guardians of our morals. Those who tell us how we go wrong and how we can improve ourselves often need a little lecturing themselves. Those who give strong advice and strong medicine seldom take it themselves.

Dream great, dream beautiful.
Build castles in the air.
And put foundations under them.

I know a college principal, an upright man, who constantly criticized his students and even his staff for their indolence, incompetence, indiscipline, insolence, ineffectiveness, ineptitude, and inevitable failure in life, all the time being totally oblivious to the moral ineptitude of his own eighteen-year-old son, who was usually to be found in bars and gambling dens, dispensing the family fortunes on wine and women, if not song. He came to a terrible end, but not before he had destroyed both his own and his father's reputation. But the fault lay with the self-important parent who faulted others while being blind to the flaws of his own flesh and blood.

So, I do not lecture or give advice. Be true to yourself, true to your nature; that's all I can say. Our friend W. Shakespeare said it better:

✹✹

This above all:
To thine own self be true;
And it must follow, as the night the day,
Thou canst not then be false to any man.

✹✹

My father inscribed these words in my autograph album when I was nine. They still ring true.

During my school years, I usually placed second in class exams. My chief rival was a German boy, Kasper Kirschner, who was brilliant in science and mathematics, two subjects in which I was relatively weak, to say the least. This used to bother me at first, but then I consoled myself with the thought that I would be a writer (or work on anything to do with books or language), leaving the scientific field wide open for Kasper. While it is good to come first in an exam or a race, it is also good to come second or third. Don't let it get you down.

We were good friends, Kasper and I, although we came from very different backgrounds. During the war years, he, his young brother and his parents had been prisoners-of-war

WHILE IT IS GOOD TO COME FIRST IN AN EXAM OR A RACE, IT IS ALSO GOOD TO COME SECOND OR THIRD.

in a detention camp outside Dehradun—the same internment camp from which Heinrich Harrer (a fellow prisoner) escaped and made his way to Tibet, later to write his best-selling book, Seven Years in Tibet. My father had served in the RAF during the war, so Kasper and I were really on opposite sides—or had been—in those tumultuous times. But it made no difference to our friendship. We discussed books, films, sports, world affairs and played football together.

When we passed out of school, I went to England, and Kasper went back to Germany. He concentrated on his studies and, in time, became a professor of biology at Basel University in Switzerland. I did not go to college, but I did make my way as a writer. First or second, it did not matter—we both did what we had set out to do. Over the years, we stayed in touch and met again a few years ago when he came to these parts on a trekking expedition. A boyhood rivalry had cemented into a lifelong friendship.

As schoolboys, both Kasper and I focused on what we wanted to do in life, and I think that helped us overcome obstacles and setbacks along the way. We stayed true to our natures.

* * *

Don't run, walk. Or, conversely, walk, don't run.

The first sentence sounds like an order, while the next one sounds like a suggestion. And I believe in suggestions, not orders. I can go along with a suggestion, but I resent an order. So do most people, unless they are raw army recruits who would be well advised to snap to attention.

DON'T RUN,
WALK.
OR, CONVERSELY,
WALK,
DON'T RUN.

Running after something you desire often creates an elusive target or prey. It is better to let it come to you, as it will if you are any good. Love, success, happiness and wealth are inclined to take fright and vanish if you pursue them too ferociously. The bee or the butterfly must come to the flower. The flower doesn't have to go anywhere.

There are just a few good reasons for running.

* **One:** If you want to save someone from drowning. In which case, you should be able to swim. Otherwise, run for help.

* **Two:** If you are an athlete desirous of winning a race or a ball player of some kind who endeavours to score a goal or run after a ball. (For this reason, I was a goalkeeper, not much running about.)

* **Three:** If you are being chased by an angry bull, it is best to run. If you are being chased by a tiger, don't bother running unless you happen to be Usain Bolt. When I was a boy, my ayah told me that if ever I met a tiger,

I should call it 'uncle', and it would not harm me. (I have not yet had the opportunity to prove or disprove her theory.)

Are there any other good reasons for running?

If a bomb goes off in the street, everyone runs in panic. But that's different. Disaster creates panic, and when we panic, we run. We make for the safest place. It's the law of self-protection.

I have always preferred walking—more for pleasure than for profit. I have walked in the hills, and I have walked in the plains. The best way to get to know a town or city is to walk all over it. As a young man, I walked all over London, from Primrose Hill to Regent's Park, from Mile End Road to Limehouse and the docks and from Lambeth to Kew Gardens.

In New Delhi, in my twenties, I used to walk from Connaught Place (CP) in central Delhi to Rajouri Gardens in the west on a winter's evening, consuming boiled eggs along the way. And on a Sunday afternoon, I would walk from CP to the Red Fort—it was just a stroll. But there wasn't much traffic in those days. I wouldn't attempt it today. Not that I can walk very far at the age of ninety. But there's Rakesh, Siddharth and Shrishti to drive me around.

Just last week, we went for a drive along the Tekri Road; the same road I crossed on foot some fifty years ago, walking from Mussoorie to Chamba. Half a century ago, it was a footpath or mule track, and sometimes you did not see a human for miles. Now, of course, it's a popular drive for tourists, presenting magnificent views to both north and south—the higher ranges on one side, the valleys stretching away on the other. Pine and deodar, and here and there, a rhododendron tree, blooming in March or April, depending on the mood of the weather gods.

We stopped at a small wayside hamlet called Baras-Khanda. ('Baras' means rhododendron, and 'Khanda' means hillside.) It's early November, and there are no flowers, although the owner of a small restaurant has managed to grow some geraniums on his verandah, and they are colourful and welcoming. You can't go wrong with geraniums if you know where to plant them. They need both sun and shelter, and they hate the wind—hot winds as well as cold winds, both are anathema to geraniums.

But you don't want to know about geraniums. You want to know about the happy day, the perfect day that came about without any planning or great expectations.

Don't plan for a happy day; just let it happen. A happy disposition probably has something to do with it. If you are a cheerful person inherently, you will naturally gravitate towards what is pleasing to behold and what uplifts your spirits. Look for the rainbow, even when rainbows are out of season. There is always something else up in the sky.

We heard a distant honking, not of car horns but of wild ducks. Looking up, I saw formations of them flying south, escaping the Siberian cold for the warm marshlands of the Indian plains.

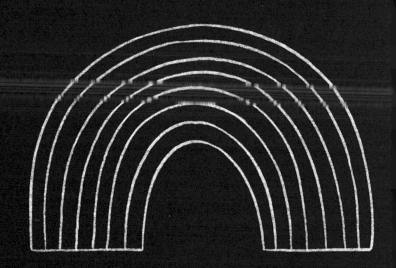

Look for the

RAINBOW,

even when rainbows
are out of season.

An inspiring sight—certainly more inspiring than the televised pictures of Russian or Israeli tanks making for the battleground. I have never been a serious birdwatcher (being reluctant to get out of bed before sunrise), but I have always found birdwatchers to be well-balanced people. They have come, quite rightly, to the conclusion that birds are the most beautiful creatures in the world, and they want to see as many of them as possible.

If only geraniums grew from guns and ducks and geese roamed the skies instead of fighter jets, this world would be what it was intended to be—great, wide and beautiful, with land and sea providing enough for all.

We are born with our natures, and it is hard to change them.

Shrishti is always bubbling over with laughter and high spirits, while Deepak, her cousin, seldom smiles and doesn't have much to say about anything. He has always been like that.

I am a bit of a pessimist myself, always expecting the worst. My imagination visualizes disasters of every kind. And so, when things go well, the relief is wonderful, and I am all joy and optimism!

Well, no two people are the same. One brother may have a vicious temper, while the other is gentle as a lamb. For that matter, no two dogs or cats are the same.

Mimi, sitting here behind the geraniums, is patiently waiting for me to vacate the chair so that she can have her share of the sun.

She hasn't quite forgiven me for accidentally sitting on her yesterday. She now looks at me with an air of tolerant superiority. I am, after all, just a blundering human.

✳ ✳ ✳

Old soldiers never die; they simply fade away, or so the saying goes. And what about writers? Well, old writers never die—they simply go out of print.

In print or out, we carry on writing. That is, if we are born writers—writers by nature, given to self-expression through the medium of the written word.

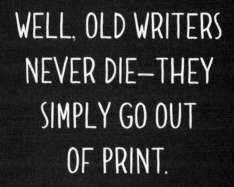

WELL, OLD WRITERS
NEVER DIE—THEY
SIMPLY GO OUT
OF PRINT.

The creative instinct is in our genes, and those of us who possess it go on to make beautiful paintings, music or poetry. Indeed, we must put our creative potential to good use if we are not to throw away this gift of life.

****

Ars longa, vita brevis.

****

Loosely translated, it means art is long and life is short. Michelangelo is still with us; so is Beethoven, and so are the Marx Brothers. Even Father Time must yield to true genius. And because life is short (compared to the millions of years in time past), we must seize it by the coattails and hang on for all we are worth because it can so easily slip away and leave us alone on the beach, looking for seashells. It is better to look for pearls than shells, but even shells are beautiful. As a child, I collected them, marvelling at the intricacies of their designs, some smooth as glass, others encrusted with the patterns of the ocean's small creatures. Everything that is not man-made is, in its own way, perfect—the mollusc, the

starfish, the crab, the oyster, the swordfish, the octopus, the whale and the treasures yet to be discovered. In many ways, the sea is still a mystery, but our attention is being diverted by the earth and the stars.

Although I have spent most of my life in the mountains and often write about them, the literature of the sea has always fascinated me! The stories of Joseph Conrad (who understood the sea better than anyone), Stevenson (who romanticized it), R.H. Dana Jr (who lived with it), Maugham (who roamed over it), W.W. Jacobs

(who found humour in it), and of course Melville (who revered it) and gave us an idea of the sea's true stature in Moby Dick.

Oddly enough, I cannot, at the moment, think of any great 'mountain literature'. Perhaps because the mountains are fixed, and the sea flows, taking us here and there. Well, there was Knut Hamsun in Norway and B. Traven in Mexico's Sierra Madre—both great writers. No doubt you can tell me of others. Second to the sea, it is probably the desert that has been celebrated the most through the written word, mostly by travellers who used their five senses wherever they went—C.M. Doughty,

Freya Stark, T.E. Lawrence (in Arabia), Peter Fleming (in Central Asia), Wilfred Thesiger (among the Marsh Arabs). It takes great observers and great writers to do justice to the desert.

In the time given to you, my friends, read as much as you can. Relish and absorb the thoughts and feelings of these men and women who recorded their experiences of a wonderful world that is still here—but might indeed disappear if we are too careless with it.

We are gifted with five senses—sight, sound, smell, taste and touch. Let's use them to get the most out of life. They will give you all the sensations you want without recourse to drugs or other stimulants.

'The eyes have it.' They take prominence, as they did in one of my earliest stories, which went by that name. We need our eyes to find our way, indoors and out, or when stopping by the wayside to admire a beautiful bird, delicate flower or transient butterfly. We need our eyes for the pleasures of reading and the excitement of writing. We need them to look upon our fellow creatures—humans as odd as ourselves, animals and birds and insects as

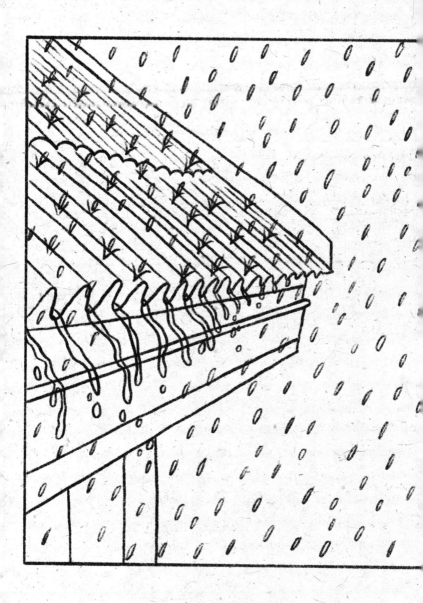

perfect as nature made them. We need our eyes to gaze upon the miracles of this planet— and to avoid tripping over some of them.

Then there's our sense of hearing. 'What big ears you have!' said Little Red Riding Hood to the big wolf disguised as her grandmother. Do big ears hear better than small ears? I've no idea. We'll have to ask the elephants. Or the snakes who hear well enough without ears. My uncle Ken had big ears, but he wasn't too bright. So, let's just say that some sounds are worth hearing—bird song and the rustle of spring—and some are troublesome, such as loudspeakers relaying political harangues or wedding music floating into a small house.

The sense of smell enables us to enjoy the fragrance of the rose, the jasmine and the honeysuckle. But there are also smells we could do without, including the pungent odour of polluted air. Our sense of smell is now attuned to the urban environment, and obnoxious smells are fast becoming the norm.

But there's still the sense of taste, and that's something over which we still have some control. And the sense of touch—that too is ours still. The touch of a loving hand—that gentle touch on a fevered brow; the clasp of a father's hand . . .

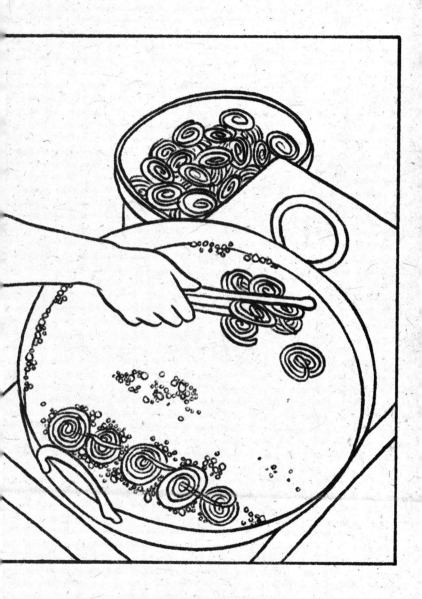

As a small boy, with my hand in my father's, I was taken for long nature walks in search of rare butterflies and beetles . . . the years fall away as I remember and still feel the grasp of that guiding hand.

Only yesterday, as I dozed off in this sunny corner where I write, I felt a soft touch on my cheek. I opened my eyes to see Shrishti standing there with my favourite drink, a strawberry milkshake, as only she can make it. Three senses mingled together—sight, taste, touch—what could be more perfect?

❋ ❋ ❋

Kindness is all. It's a great gift. If you can go through life being kind to people (and animals), you will be blessed with a happy and contented nature. The road to happiness consists of making others happy—of taking only a tiny slice of cake so that your friend or partner (or even a stranger) can enjoy the larger slice.

Kindness lifts us above the level of the beast. It is the one thing that justifies our claim to being civilized beings. Be kind to those you love; be kind to those who work with you or for you; be kind to children, old people, those who have fallen from grace, those who have given up trying to succeed and those who have done

KINDNESS
IS ALL.

their best and failed, for you and I might be one of them.

Be kind to creatures both wild and domestic—the gentle gazelle, the homely cow, the water-loving buffalo, the long-suffering camel, the crafty crow, the industrious tailorbird, the generous egg-laying hen, the agile elephant, the fallen sparrow, the wounded tiger, the brave ant, the elegant heron, the scuttling crab, the leaping frog, the timid mouse . . .

Just yesterday, a skink, a harmless little reptile, was seeking shelter under the rubber plant climbing my bedroom wall. This plant has been my guest for over twenty years and is still flourishing. Beena wanted to throw the skink out of the window, but I said to let it be. (I told her skinks bring luck. Beena is even more superstitious than I am!) But if I want the skink to survive, I shall have to keep it hidden from my cat, Mimi, who shows no mercy towards smaller creatures.

Mimi has her own views on mice and frogs and skinks, and I respect her views, even if they differ from mine. We have one thing in common, though: a likeness for sardines—they come in tins before I can save them! Well, we can't be perfect.

I have led an imperfect life, but I have done my best, for myself and for those I love.

We can't be perfect, but we can strive for perfection, and in the process, we might do something worthwhile.

So, hang on to your dreams, my young friends. Don't give up on them. They keep us going, and along the way, there are many pleasant diversions.

Be kind, my friends. Be wise and strong, and do not take from anyone their dream, their song.

Ruskin Bond,

Among the geraniums

December 2023

AFTERWORD

But there are no afterwards. Only new beginnings. And new beginnings are the fruition of all of our dreams.

Regardless of whether you are nine or ninety, don't stop dreaming. The seasons will change, the world will turn. At ninety, I'm dreaming of peach blossom in the Spring, of mangoes in the Summer, of lemons in winter. I dream of writing new and better stories — and sometimes I write them! I dream of writing poems celebrating the beauties of nature — and sometimes I write them. I dream of writing about old friends, old roads, lost gardens — and sometimes I write about them! I don't let my dreams run away from me. I make them work for me. So hold on to your dreams. Never let them go!

Ruskin Bond
March, 2024

ACKNOWLEDGEMENTS

Many thanks to Samar Bansal for his designs, Pearl D'souza for her illustrations, and Sohini and Shabari from the Penguin editorial team for making this a dream of a book.

Scan QR code to access the
Penguin Random House India website